the four goals of life
a survival guide for the kali yuga

Cynkay Morningsong, M.A.
©2012

Copyright © 2012

All rights reserved

ISBN:147507946X

ISBN-13: 978-1475079463

To my Guru…

Family…

Friends…

I bow to you all in gratitude for your love and support!

Contents

- A Survival Guide for the Kali Yuga ... 5
  - Dharma ... 14
    - Physical ... 21
    - Mental/Emotional ... 25
    - Spiritual ... 29
  - Artha ... 33
    - Physical ... 41
    - Mental ... 45
    - Spiritual ... 49
  - Kama ... 56
    - Physical ... 64
    - Mental ... 70
    - Spiritual ... 75
- Moksha ... 82
  - Physical ... 87
  - Mental ... 92
  - Spiritual ... 96
- Synergy ... 100
- Resources ... 104

the four goals of life: a survival guide for the kali yuga

The life of Brahma is eternal. We live in a universe filled with objects and relationships in which we, although eternal beings, are moving about in temporary bodies. We have forgotten that our true nature is Divine and that we are, as manifestations from the creative mind of Brahma, eternal. We have become deluded by the sensory world, we've forgotten our True Nature, and we have come to identify ourselves with the temporary world in which we reside.

Although this book is subtitled *A Survival Guide for the Kali Yuga*, I am going to begin by explaining why we may or may not be living in the time of the Kali Yuga. One advantage to starting here is that it allows me to set a context for this book and explain some important technicalities, before moving on to the Guide itself.

Although Brahma's eternal life is never ending, we divide eternity into various understandable and comprehensible segments. These divisions include minutes, hours, days, months, years, decades, centuries, and a less familiar term – yugas. All of these divisions help us to keep track of events and set a context for our lives. They are important agreements for keeping us engaged in the present as they define the moment we are experiencing now, and its relationship to life as a whole.

We know that the planets of our solar system are in rotation around the sun, but our sun is also believed to be rotating another greater, more powerful, star at the center of the galaxy. The length of time it takes for our sun to complete its orbit around this galactic center is calculated at 24,000 years, equal to one day in the life of Brahma.

The ascending phase of our rotation, from the farthest point away from galactic center to the nearest, is 12,000 years, as is the descending phase. The ascending phase is a day of Brahma; the descending phase is the night. Each of these is divisible into 4 *yugas* or ages.

These yugas include the Satya, Treta, Dwapara, and the Kali Yuga.

The yuga known as the *Satya Yuga* is comprised of 4000 years and also has 400 transition years (called *sandhis)* before and after, for a total of 4800 years. The *Treta Yuga* is 3000 years, and in like manner, also includes 300 sandhis before and after, the *Dwapara Yuga* of 2000 years with 200 before and after, and the *Kali Yuga* which lasts 1000 years with 100 years on either side, thus a night equaling 12,000 years. As we ascend back to the nearest point of our rotation we go through these yugas again, this time in reverse: Kali, Dwapara, Treta, and Satya.

According to Sri Yukteswar Giri, well known as the Guru of Paramahansa Yogananda, the current rotation began around 11,501 B.C. as our sun began to rotate away from galactic center, thus beginning the descending Satya Yuga, the age of truth. As we continued to move through time and the Treta and Dwapara yugas we also moved further and further away from the earlier golden age. When we began the descending Kali yuga in 699 b.c. we were in such ignorance and darkness that scholars who were able to calculate, or willing to identify, our entrance into the Kali Yuga were unavailable; and so it was widely believed that we were still in the Dwapara yuga past the time in which we actually were.

According to these calculations we entered the ascending Dwapara Yuga in 1699 a.d. and completed the sandhi in 1899, currently putting us at around 112 years into the Dwapara Yuga itself. This date correlates with the many technological advances that we are experiencing. Although we have moved on cosmologically, in many ways we continue to notice and experience the spiritual ignorance that typifies the Kali Yuga. We are still early into the Age of Yoga, and haven't yet shaken ourselves completely awake.

What are the signs of the Kali Yuga? According to Wikipedia:

Attributes of Kali Yuga

A discourse by Markandeya in the Mahabharata identifies some of the attributes of Kali Yuga:

In relation to rulers

- Rulers will become unreasonable: they will levy taxes unfairly.

- Rulers will no longer see it as their duty to promote spirituality, or to protect their subjects: they will become a danger to the world.

- People will start migrating, seeking countries where wheat and barley form the staple food source.

In human relationships

- Avarice and wrath will be common. Humans will openly display animosity towards each other.

- Ignorance of dharma will occur.

- People will have thoughts of murder with no justification and will see nothing wrong in that.

- Lust will be viewed as socially acceptable and sexual intercourse will be seen as the central requirement of life.

- Sin will increase exponentially, whilst virtue will fade and cease to flourish.

- People will take vows and break them soon after.

- People will become addicted to intoxicating drinks and drugs.

- Gurus will no longer be respected and their students will attempt to injure them. Their teachings will be insulted, and followers of Kama will wrest control of the mind from all human beings. Brahmins will not be learned or honored, Kshatriyas will not be brave, and Vaishyas will not be just in their dealings.

Looking at this list in relation to our current worldly conditions clearly shows why many believe we are still in the Kali Yuga. While all of these characteristics were very much in place during the 2400 years of the descending & ascending Kali Yuga, we seem to still be tangled in the web of many of these qualities. The Kali Yuga has led us into such darkness that we find it difficult to un-stick ourselves from it.

However, in the Dwapara Yuga it is our dharma to reach for unity. During this period we begin to remember that we are One by focusing on unity and learning to relate to life without the illusion of separation. We'll grow in the understanding that what we have perceived as matter is, in fact, energy and the vibrations of particles. We aim to overcome avidya and maya, spiritual ignorance and illusion, and evolve into a quantum give and take, universal reality that is aligned with Spiritual Law.

Aitareya Brahmana said:

One who lies down is Kali
One who awakens is Dwapara
One who stands up becomes Treta
And one who moves on realizes the Satya Yuga.
Therefore move on!

The Kali Yuga is known as the age of darkness. I like to think of the Dwapara Yuga as the age of Yoga. To make the most of our time here, we must focus on moving beyond the belief that we are separate from each other and Spirit, and find new ways of uniting and creating balance within ourselves, our communities, and our relationship with God. In 1893 this current Yuga began with Swami Vivekananda's presentation at the Parliament of the World's Religions in Chicago. His arrival in America was at the beginning of the Dwapara Yuga, further confirming the timing of our shift from Kali to Dwapara.

While we are still experiencing the outdated residual effects of the previous Kali Yuga, more and more we are opening up to an innovative, community building, brighter and more unitive, current age. The unrest and upheaval we see in our current day's worldwide political and financial systems show us that we truly are moving into a time of increasing community and enlightenment. No longer are we willing to settle for what someone else thinks is best, we want to create a world that works for everyone.

We are here in this world, during this time, in order to wake up to that which we are – drops of water in the Ocean of Mercy. Just as a drop taken from the ocean is still ocean, but not The Ocean, we are drops of Divinity, but not the entirety of what is Divine. When we believe that we are the entire Ocean, or forget that we already are *pure* Ocean, we become caught in the intertwining web of *maya* – illusion, and *moha* – confusion.

It is recommended that we lead a balanced life with an ultimate goal. One way in which Sanatana Dharma suggests we accomplish this is through the achievement of the purusharthas – the four goals of life. Goals are necessary in every aspect of our lives. As Swami Satyananda Saraswati (Swamiji) teaches we must always keep our "goals" in mind so that when we "wander off" into confusion, or get stuck in delusion, our regular practice will bring us back to wholeness. Then, refreshed and revitalized, we again go into the world." Swamiji says: "without a goal, we become part of someone else's plan."

The purpose of this book is to offer the reader a roadmap to understanding how to move oneself along the path from the dark consciousness of the Kali Yuga and into the light of the Dwapara Yuga. Here we find words offering us a method of moving out of the age of darkness so that we might enter fully and consciously into a well balanced, purposeful, hopeful, light-filled, awakening to our Divine Nature. I've chosen to do this by examining life's four goals of Dharma, Artha, Kama, & Moksha. These goals include all of the primary activities we participate in and that all of us are here to achieve.

Let's consider that Dharma is *what you do,* Artha is *what you have,* Kama is *what you want,* and Moksha is *freedom from separation.*

We pursue each of these goals throughout our lives. The goals we haven't yet accomplished will impact our success in achieving the other goals now, as well as carry on with us into future lifetimes. Putting our conscious attention on the attainment of our goals allows us to understand where our work is. They interact with each other and are interdependent and mutually inclusive. For example: If you are not achieving your goals for Artha (wealth) it may be a result of not following your purpose in life (Dharma) or because you are making poor relationship choices (Kama). It is difficult to put our attention on Self-Realization (Moksha) when challenges managing goals regarding our life purpose keep us focused on the satisfaction of basic needs. By keeping our perspective open to noticing where we are out of balance, we find that we are better able to keep life in perspective.

Sri Yashpal Singh said: "We should soar in this world like a bird whose body is made up of Dharma or principles, and who moves toward the spiritual goal of Moksha or Liberation by balanced use of the two wings of Artha (monetary pursuits) and Kama (emotional and social pursuits)."

I will address each goal separately, defining them, applying them to our physical, mental/emotional, and spiritual experience of life. As this will be presented from an Ayurvedic perspective I'll also use the Science of Life to suggest remedial measures intended to assist the reader in finding balance in the objects and relationships of their experience.

The first of these goals, or principle's of right living, is the goal of Dharma. According to Merriam-webster.com, Dharma means: life purpose, duty according to custom, law, or nature; divine law; basic principles of cosmic or personal existence.

Each of us chose to incarnate during this time in order to fulfill a purpose in life along with our karmic obligations. We have received all of the gifts and talents that are best suited to the fulfillment of our individual

Dharma, and in doing so we join together to fulfill our collective Dharma. A challenge we are faced with in following our Dharma is that most of us are not encouraged to explore and develop our gifts. We are not taught that we are each a unique and nonreplicable manifestation in the mind of Brahma, believing instead that it is better for us to "hide our light under a bushel" and blend in with our neighbors and peers. While we do reward certain types of excellence on a cultural level, for most of us who are not superstars, yet still fully actualizing our Dharma, the rewards will be internal and personal.

Our Dharma is very much about our relationship to ourselves and our role in the world. What are we known for? What career have we chosen? Are we trustworthy, efficient, and do we take care of our physical body and surroundings? Dharma is what we do in the world; thus, it includes our work, our families, and all of our other activities. Dharma also includes our internal motivators such as integrity, drive, compassion, and ethics. It is our heritage and the circumstances of our lives.

Unless we begin by addressing our purpose in life from a perspective in which we consider our Dharma, little else in our experience will produce the fruits of our effort. We must be willing and committed to follow our Dharma. We have all known of a person whose parents or society wanted him to become a doctor or lawyer, yet the child really just wanted to play piano, paint, or study mathematics (or any other vocation.) If we are prevented from following our Dharma we find it difficult to encourage others in following theirs; or we may become attached to encouraging them to follow ours. If we don't follow our Dharma we will often live with the feeling that something is "missing" from our lives.

Not following through on the opportunities we are presented with in life is another way in which we miss the mark and find ourselves having difficulty when it comes to achieving our goals. Many times we hold our true purpose at arm's length because we are afraid we might not succeed! But truly, how could we not succeed at what we are here to do? Dharma is purpose and action; as well as intention and integrity. It is our destiny and what we have to offer society. Dharma allows us to influence the world through our thoughts and associations. It is the action that we take in life. We consider ourselves to be a failure when life doesn't work out in the ways we had expected it to; however, our expectations and desires are not necessarily in the best interest of our greatest good. What we might consider a failure is very likely to become one of our greatest gifts in life.

Even when we don't like how life is appearing today we can certainly know that everything always works out fine in the end. However difficult and traumatic today is, the challenges we are faced with that may seem overwhelming in this moment will certainly resolve themselves in some way that will contribute to our personal growth and ability to meet life with ever increasing strength and understanding.

This brings to mind a song on the environmental children's music recording titled *At Night they Howl at the Moon* by John Seed & Dana Lyons that I had for my children in the early 90's. The song "No More Bunya Nuts" has a line that says "Dharma is the things you do, Karma is what comes to you." Most of us are familiar with the word karma and understand it's meaning to be something like cause and effect. If we do something bad, we'll receive bad in return. Actually, everything that we do creates karma. We are *jiva* "embodied souls" and therefore trapped within the cycle of our karma.

We are here to manifest and fulfill our parabdha karma which consists of the actions we've taken in the past that are now, and in the future, bearing the fruit of our experience. We are constantly creating new karma's for ourselves; just as we will create other karma's to work out in the future; a seemingly never ending cycle! Our goal then, as our karma relates to our dharma, is to stay as much on purpose as possible. Dharma is how we fulfill our karmic debts. Using discrimination in our choices allows us to respond to life, rather than react to it. When we are able to do that we find the freedom to be unattached to our preferred outcomes, and free to act in the most appropriate way at any given time.

When you find yourself believing that someone is "doing" something to you remember that we are all instruments of each other's karma. Since we are all One, all part of a larger than our little personal lives organism, all Brahma - everything that takes place in front of us is part of a bigger experience then we are aware of. Usually we don't even know the full extent of our actions on the rest of life. This shows us what a disservice to all of creation not fulfilling one's Dharma is. Life is much more than our personal experience and individual understanding of it. We have a responsibility, not only to ourselves but to the world, that we manifest our Dharma to the best of our ability. Fulfillment of our Dharma expresses and maintains the unity of creation. It is how Spirit uses each of Its tools (us) to manifest all that is.

Our Dharma is that which supports us and maintains our interdependence with the world. It is an internal support and at the essence of our being. Our Dharma is our integrity and righteousness. We each have our own personal rulebook containing the guiding beliefs behind our choices, relationships, and behaviors. If something is unacceptable to me, according to my rules, it is very unlikely that I will be able to tolerate that behavior in my association with you. This is a major communication difficulty many of us have. If we are unwilling, afraid, or otherwise unable to communicate that our personal Dharma requires a particular action, we will be angry with those who don't comply with our personal rules; when in fact, the problem is our own and no one else's.

The idea of caste is related to Dharma. A caste is a method used to distinguish social divisions. While the caste system, due to the Kali Yuga, has very negative connotations for many, I would like to look at it from the perspective of astrology. There are four castes in all: Brahmin, Kshatriya, Vaishya, and Shudra. Brahmins are concerned with universal law and the relationship between mankind and God - Moksha. Kshatriyas place their attention upon defining the best course of action - Dharma, Vaishyas with material goods - Artha, and Shudras with basic needs - Kama.

Vedic astrology is very much concerned with understanding our Dharma and can be quite helpful in determining the Dharma of an individual, especially when their earlier conditioning in life has sustained the veils of maya and moha. The houses in our birth chart that are specific to understanding our Dharma include the 1st, 5th, & 9th. The 10th is also important as the karma bhava and is useful in showing us the specific ways in which we might fulfill our Dharma as it related to our career or profession.

The first house shows us the qualities of our physical bodies, along with the challenges and blessings we may experience in that domain of our lives. The fifth house shows our progeny, or that which we will give birth to, and other creative pursuits. The ninth house often indicates our father and the forces that brought us to this lifetime, but it can also signify our fate and wisdom as well as higher learning and our religious disposition. That, combined with the 10th house qualities of respect and fame, prestige, and advancement in our affairs, offers us much in terms of understanding our Dharma.

A qualified astrologer can be very helpful in determining our Dharma when we have become confused by all of the opportunities we are faced with.

physical

How do we follow our Dharma on a physical level? What is our purpose? What motivates us to live out our goals regarding that purpose?

When it comes to fulfilling our Dharma very little will serve us better than to create and maintain a healthy, balanced lifestyle. A first step in this is to determine our Ayurvedic Dosha as an understanding of the elements driving our experience and expression in life will help us to make choices that are appropriate for us.

The doshas are the three humors which make up the constitution of humans and the world around us. We are each a combination of all three doshas. These include Vata – air-ether/wind, Pitta – fire-water/bile, and Kapha – earth-water/phlegm. Most of us are primarily an active blend of two or three doshas; it is the rare individual who is solely influenced by only one. According to Tri-doshic theory, all disease is a result of these humors being out of balance, with vata dosha being the dosha primarily deranged in most disease processes.

We have a primary constitution or prakriti, and a secondary constitution or vikriti. Our prakriti shows us our nature, and vikriti shows whether prakriti is in balance. Vata affects the empty spaces within our bodies such as bones, hollow organs, nerves, and colon. Diseases such as arthritis, bowel diseases and the absorption of nutrients, as well as conditions of the nervous system are all vata related. Vata is the force that creates movement in the body. As we age we become more prone to vata related disturbances and we see the incidence of vata diseases increase.

Pitta is bile and the element of our internal fire - *Agni,* which is required for the metabolism of nutrients. Pitta resides in the bile producing organs of the liver and spleen as well as in our heart, eyes, and skin. Whatever we take into our body, and is then transformed into nourishment, is acted upon by Pitta dosha; it is the transformative power of our body. It is also our intensity of thought and activity. Pitta is vital to fulfilling our purpose in life as it provides us with the drive, determination and motivation to strive for our excellence.

Kapha dosha involves the fluids and other lubricants within our bodies including lymph, phlegm, reproductive fluids, and fat. It is the provider of stability and accumulation, and is the dosha of growth. If we were to compare our body with that of a plant kapha would reside in the roots; pitta in the oils, resins, and sap; and we would find vata in the leaves, stems, flowers, and fruit.

Knowing the impact of the doshas is helpful if we are to create a life that is healthy and in balance. When determining our purpose in life vata creates within us the question, pitta the motivation to do what is necessary to our fulfillment and kapha the stability and endurance to follow through and continue, even when challenges occur. Hatha yoga can be useful in discovering our Dharma. As we spend time on the mat, exploring the range of our motions and emotions, we find clarity regarding our purpose in life. This clarity then leads us to a deeper understanding of our intentions and goals along with greater success in the fulfillment of our purpose.

How do we know what our purpose is? This is a question we are all faced with. Many people, unhappy with their current work and feeling as if something vital is missing in their lives, turn to harmful practices and addictions in an attempt to fill the void resulting from not finding and committing to what they have embodied in order to accomplish. You can discover your purpose by looking to your own life for the answers. What do you love to do? What is it that brings you the greatest satisfaction? What are your goals? What is important to you?

Sometimes, if we are not clear on our purpose, it can be helpful to ask ourselves; "if money were not an issue, what would I do with my life?" Another good question might be; "what do I want to be remembered for?" Either of these questions can be a doorway into our stored away dreams and gifts.

There is a Bach Flower Remedy called "wild oat" which is helpful in stimulating our connection to our life purpose. Flower essences work on very subtle levels and help us to connect with our subconscious specifically through our connection with the natural world.

Chakras are energy centers found within our subtle body and aligned with our physical spine. The chakra's most involved in our life purpose include the first chakra: the root or muladhara located at the base of the perineum, and the third chakra: the solar plexus or manipura chakra which correlates with the area behind the navel. We can connect to the energies of these chakras through various guided meditations and visualizations. The aroma of essential oils bring balance to our chakras as well; sandalwood and frankincense for the muladhara, rosemary and chamomile for the manipura. The first chakra responds to the color red, and yellow will to activate and nourish the third chakra.

mental/emotional

Personal experience puts each of us at the center of our personal cosmology. We even have our own myths and stories about the events in our lives. Our understanding of an experience is unique to each of us. Even when more than one person shares in the encounter, we will each have a different memory of what happened that is layered upon all of the beliefs and past events influencing our understanding and experience. The story is always told from our own perspective, given our own meaning, and with ourselves cast as the star. The universe revolves around me, just as it revolves around you.

Although we are told throughout our lives not to be "selfish" the truth is that being "self-ish" simply means to be more consistently our selves. Would we ask the sky to stop being blue-ish? No more than we would insist that a forest refrain from being green-ish. Looked at in this way, to be Self-ish, may be the highest and truest expression of our life!

Being at the center of the universe does have its problems and consequences however. Permission to believe that the cosmos is revolving around us can cause difficulty when we forget that everyone else is also at the center of the universe, we aren't the only person whose concerns are of significance! Unless we are considering the impact on the entire system as a whole we are acting out of ego & separation (*avidya*), rather than from the intelligent understanding of unity and consciousness - *vidya*. While there is certainly one universe (that we are consciously aware of) the center of the universe – Mount Meru, is the spinal support within each of us.

We also get into trouble when we attempt to make someone else the center of our lives. While others may believe, perhaps even insist that they want to be the center of your life - in truth nobody really wants this. It is impossible to follow your own Dharma when someone has given you responsibility for theirs as well. This occurs when we get into the habit of reacting, rather than responding. When we make an effort to act out our lives from a sense of purpose we will always respond in the best possible way to the world around us. Responding is an appropriate reply when our universe offers us changing conditions. Reacting is something we do unconsciously and habitually.

Fortunately, precedent is not principle. Just because we have reacted in certain specific ways in the past does not imply that we are bound to always responding in the same way as future events unfold. As we become aware of our Dharma, and commit to where it will lead us, we have the opportunity to respond in new and innovative ways.

The Gunas are energetic *bhavas*, or feelings, that assist us in better understanding our human experience. There are three gunas. The first is Sattva – which is calm, peaceful, and clear. Sattvic food is nourishing and easily digestible, typically on the sweet side. One of my favorite Sattvic foods is Organic Raw Whey Powder. This food is so clearly nourishing that even holding the container one can feel the energetic goodness of the food. It is like concentrated sunshine! The Sun nourished the grass which nourished the cow that gave us the milk. Sattvic foods also include plant based fresh foods such as fruits, vegetables and pure water.

The second guna is Rajas. Rajasic energy is frenetic and tumultuous, but also passionate and creative. It can be very intense and lead us to act rashly and impetuously. This is the energy of desire and ambition that can also lead us to competition and over stimulation. Imagine the color red and you will feel the energy of rajas. Coffee, onions, peppers, many spices, and alcohol are all examples of Rajasic foods.

Finally we have Tamas. Tamasic energy is the energy of inertia and rest. It can also be dull, lifeless, lazy and greedy. When we have done too much Rajasic activity we find ourselves thrust into Tamas in order to recover. Tamasic behavior can be unconscious and destructive, but also regenerative and recuperative. All addictive behaviors are Tamasic, even when they give the appearance, or are reputed to be of Sattva or Rajas Guna. Foods that are Tamasic include meat and anything stale, reheated, canned, or foods that are overly ripe. These foods have little or no life energy left in them. Not only are they unable to sustain a healthy life, they also contribute to disease.

The goal is to balance the gunas in order that we can move more into the bhava of Sattva. We do this by seeking to eliminate those substances, behaviors, and thoughts that serve to keep us agitated or numb.

Understanding which of the guna's are more actively influencing our lives can lead us to a better understanding of our Dharma and clearly show us whether we are fulfilling our purpose in life. If we believe that our purpose is to do a certain thing, yet our experience is one of uncomfortable intensity, or we feel dull and lifeless while doing it, it is probably not part of our life's purpose. On the other hand, if our work brings us joy, peace, and satisfaction we can be assured of being on the right path.

spiritual

Ultimately, our purpose in life is Self-Realization and we will address this more thoroughly when we discuss the fourth goal – Moksha. But how do we consider Dharma from the perspective of spirituality?

The study of spiritual and universal truths from master teachers can provide us with a change in perspective, particularly when we have struggled with finding our purpose. One significant and well loved example of this is told in the Bhagavad Gita as Arjuna, man, is taught by his charioteer and friend, Lord Krishna, God, how to live his purpose.

During their discussion Krishna reveals himself as God and teaches Arjuna, and the rest of us, exactly how to go about fulfilling our Dharma.

The setting is an ancient battlefield where Arjuna is preparing to enter into an inevitable battle occurring within his own family. Knowing that this battle will result in the death of those he loves and admires, Arjuna is distraught at the idea and asks his friend to council him.

Krishna asks Arjuna what is keeping him from standing up and doing his duty, to which Arjuna replies that he is confused and has a lack of will for this fight. He asks "Is there any other way out of these problems?" This question is universal and we all, when faced with the darkest night of our soul, have asked this same question. This battle of Arjuna's is the mythic battle of good and evil and during these times we realize that walking away from life is not possible. Even when we know the right course of action we are often resistant to following it for any number of reasons.

Lord Krishna begins by reminding Arjuna that this battle, this appearance of Life, is of little consequence. There is no death and reality is eternal. The Self is immortal and cannot be destroyed. Participate in the life you have, lean into what happens; that is following your Dharma. Following our path is a resolution to seek God. Lord Krishna instructs us to center our mind, release our attachments, and free ourselves from aversions.

We are told to act from our calling to make the world a better place, not from the desire to receive, but in order to make the world better for all. Performing service to others, without attachment to the outcome of our work, is being in service to God and to the circumstances of our lives. We are taught that it is in the giving of ourselves that we will receive the greatest of gifts.

Krishna tells Arjuna that whenever Dharma declines and the purpose of life is forgotten, He is reborn to protect that which is good, destroy what is evil, and restore Dharma. God is always here with us, no matter how alone we feel, and is especially present during those times when we are faced with the decisions which seem to be about life or death.

Lord Krishna reminds us that it is better to act then to renounce. We should remember that God is everywhere residing in every person, place, and activity. Therefore, we have more opportunities to express our devotion to God when we are acting in the world. Sitting alone on our meditation cushion in a mountain cave may offer an opportunity to know God personally and without distraction, but most of us are unable to express our love in a universal way through the path of an isolated renunciate. Working without attachment to reward is a deeper form of renunciation.

Through the regular practice of meditation we gain control of our will and begin to release our attachments to material possessions. In meditation, our minds become still and unwavering in our devotion; we become free from the distractions of the material world and thus achieve our goal, unity with God. Krishna assures us that by becoming established in our practice we will become free of the delusion of separation, and find ourselves firmly entrenched on our path to Self-Realization.

We find the indwelling Atman, that part of Brahma residing within our individual hearts, through faith. Without faith in the supreme laws of life it would be impossible to dwell in the forest of Vrindavan, the home of Lord Krishna. Our faith shows up in all that we do. There is only one God. We each practice our faith and devotion according to our personal and cultural beliefs; but in reality, God is all there is, all that ever was, and all that ever will be, regardless of the names we use or the practices we follow.

To be free of our karma, in order that we may attain Self-realization, we are told to offer everything to the Lord. And just as we love God, we are also loved, equally, regardless of what we do during this lifetime. As eternal beings we are infinitely lovable and God's own children, now and always. By seeking with devotion we are assured that we will dwell in heaven forever.

Situated firmly in our faith and stilling our minds through meditation, we become free from selfish attachments or prideful delusions, and our consciousness grows beyond the concept of duality. Our lives become steady and balanced, and our Dharma becomes clearly laid out before us.

The Bhagavad Gita teaches us the five elements that are required in order to accomplish any action. These include: the body, the means, the ego, the doing of the thing itself, and the Divine will. Without all of these we cannot be successful in fulfilling our Dharma. By staying on purpose we are performing an act of devotion.

Never stray from your purpose for it is what you were born to do. When one of us fulfills our Dharma we are all blessed.

artha

What is Artha? Artha is the attainment of the resources necessary in order to fulfill our Dharma. It includes all that we have and everything that is available to us. We might think of Artha as wealth, but it also includes our goals. While money is often the first thing that comes to mind when we think of wealth, we might also consider our unique gifts & talents, education, associations, property, motivations, and all of the other resources we possess.

The resources of Artha and the accumulation of wealth provide us with the ability and freedom to devote ourselves to the pursuits of the other goals. Without Artha it would be difficult to satisfy any of them. In the physical world it is necessary to have resources available in order to care for our families and other responsibilities. If we are having difficulty acquiring the means for our survival we may find that it is impossible to grow & flourish. Imagine a garden that gets just enough water to prevent it from dying. While the plants may still have green leaves, the production of fruit and flowers is minimal. On the other hand, a garden that gets plenty of water, sunshine, and other nutrients will grow with lush and abundant abandon.

Our biggest challenge regarding Artha is that we often have the desire for much more than we need; as in all else, our goal in our attainments is moderation. We can become greedy, believing in the myth that there isn't enough for all of us; as if there is a lack of whatever we may need. We focus our attention on acquiring more and more. Our attachment to wealth, and the belief that we have a limited ability to satisfy our desires, keeps us from living out our Dharma, spending time with our families, or tithing to agencies and other organizations that are doing important work in the world that we ourselves are unable to accomplish. We work and work, letting all other parts of our lives decline as we keep our nose to the grindstone.

We have been taught the adage that money is the root of all evil; however I would propose that the problem isn't money, but our relationship to that money. Money itself is simply a means of exchanging energy in order to obtain goods or services. It allows us to keep the books balanced. When we keep our attention focused on the attainment of money, and we are attached to our resources only showing up as money, we fail to notice all of the other treasures we possess.

Money provides us with the freedom to explore our possibilities. This freedom provides us with not only the means to live a life that feels purposeful, but also with the ability to feel free from limitations and the fear of what will happen if we are unable to meet our needs. Having our needs satisfied means that we are not caught in a cycle of continuous need and seeking to fulfill those needs. This cycle of lack, and seeking to remedy that lack, prevents us from resting in the realization that everything is available to us; breaking free from this cycle is the only way in which we can truly achieve satisfaction of our desires.

Our attachment to limited beliefs regarding the resources available to us keeps us locked into an addicted state of consciousness where we force ourselves to work harder and longer. To have a balanced life it is suggested that we should spend 8 hours working, 8 hours sleeping, and 8 hours in devotional practices. If you'll recall from our previous chapter and the lessons of the Bhagavad Gita, devotional practices include anything which keeps our attention on the Divine. Perhaps another way to say this would be 8 hours on Dharma (devotional practices), 8 hours on Kama (sleep & other pleasurable past times), and with the other 8 hours on Artha (building the resources necessary to perform the other two). How would your life look if you were to adjust your time and energy to satisfy those requirements?

Another thing to consider in regards to Artha is our relationship with the natural world, as it is the true source of all our resources. There is nothing you have ever received that didn't have its origin in the earth. Keeping this vital relationship to the earth as a focus we insure that our Mother will continue to provide for us and our descendents.

Because our relationship with wealth and other resources is a strong indicator of our relationship with the natural world, when we are unable to see what we have as being of value we will also see the Earth as being of little value. It works the same in reverse as well. Those who don't consider Bhu Devi (the earth) as the source of all we have, and an invaluable resource, will have little consideration or respect for other resources.

"Earth, in which lie the sea, the river and other waters,
in which food and cornfields have come to be,
in which lives all that breathes and that moves,
may she confer on us the finest of her yield.

Earth, in which the waters, common to all,
moving on all sides, flow unfailingly, day and night,
may she pour on us milk in many streams,
and endow us with luster.

May those born of thee, O Earth,
be of our welfare, free from sickness and waste,
wakeful through a long life, we shall become bearers of
tribute to thee.

Earth, my mother, set me securely with bliss in full accord
with heaven,
O wise one, uphold me in grace and splendor."

From the Bhumi Suktam

When we look to the earth we realize that there is no lack. Just as every bee has an abundance of flowers to provide for all of its nectar needs, there is plenty to go around for all of us, or there would be with the proper management of natural resources. This is where our greatest challenge lies. We are so intent on creating wealth in terms of "money for me at the cost of your needs" we fail to understand that through appropriate resource management and good stewardship of our natural resources there would be more than enough for all seven billion of us. The only place in the world where lack exists is within our minds.

While our current socio-political system seems economically unstable, and all around us we are being inundated with the message that we are only moments away from complete disaster, it is comforting to realize that there truly is plenty for everyone. There is a solution, and the solution is to remember, and take to heart, what is written in John 17:10 of the Christian Scriptures - *and all things that are mine are thine, and thine are mine: and I am glorified in them.*

This passage encourages us to share with each other, just as God shares with us. Holding our wealth back never has, and never will, contribute to our security. There are two universal laws that address this. The first is the Law of Attraction. This Law states that what we believe, and keep our attention on, will be the very thing we find. I heard a saying once that went something like: if you watch how someone does something, you will know how they do everything. Whatever belief or activity we regularly engage in will certainly show itself over and over again. If we believe that we are surrounded by evil and hatred we will certainly find plenty of validation for these beliefs;

however, if we choose to believe in beauty & love we will find ourselves immersed in God's Ocean of Mercy.

The second Law is the Law of Circulation. This Law teaches us that growth happens through giving. If you took every nickel you earned and put it under your mattress the nickels would accumulate, but without growth. On the other hand, if you were to take those nickels and place them in an interest bearing savings account, or some other form of investment, they would grow and become greater than the sum of their parts. However, if you were to take them and offer them to an organization that works to improve worldly conditions, those nickels may create a better world for all! In the same way, using your money to improve your home or community allows your money, and your life, to increase in value. What you put into life multiplies. In fact, it simply isn't possible to expect an increase in resources of any type without putting what you have into circulation – you have to give in order to receive.

The astrological houses that signify Artha include the second, sixth, and 10th. If we consider that the second house is the house of the mind we understand that our resources are intertwined with our thoughts. We must keep our mind focused on that which we want as opposed to that which we don't want. The sixth house, the house of disease, teaches us that we must keep our bodies healthy so that we might be able to make full use of our gifts, talents, and time in order to fulfill this goal. The tenth house is our house of work, what we do, and the activities we undertake in order to increase our wealth.

physical

How do we practice Artha on a physical level? From this perspective we see that our accumulation of resources is vitally important, and I don't necessarily mean money!

Years ago I saw a movie with Patrick Swayze (PS) titled *The City of Joy*. The movie takes place in a slum of Calcutta that is poverty stricken and comprised of thieves, corrupt property owners, prostitutes, lepers, and other impoverished people. While the movie itself is excellent I was also touched by comments made by PS during an interview that I later watched.

During this interview PS was talking about which part of the movie was the most powerful for him on a personal level. Because the movie was filmed on location in the City of Joy he told how meeting the people who lived there had impacted him significantly. PS said that what had moved him the most was that in this area of abject poverty, where entire families lived in dwellings that most Americans would hesitate to park their bicycles, the people were more joyful than any he had ever met. He attributed this to the fact that they looked elsewhere for their sustenance, they seemed to understand that it wasn't having a lot of money which was important, but what is in one's heart.

The goal of Artha is to help us manifest harmony in our minds and in our lives. The Srimad Bhagavatam, another Hindu scripture, defines Artha as the *purport*. It is an object perceived with the senses, and that which we are striving for. Artha is a temporary reliever of suffering, just as Kama is. Together these two form a bridge between Dharma and Moksha.

When we don't recognize or appreciate the wealth readily available in our lives we easily fall into the belief that there is not enough. The goal is not to have all that we want, but to want all that we have. How many times do people shop to fulfill an emotional need, only to have the unopened purchase sit in a dark closet?

One purpose of the purusharthas is to keep us from obsessing on desires and instead keep our focus on our obligations. According to the Taittriya Samhita we are each born with three debts that must be repaid during our lifetimes. The first debt is the debt we owe to God for providing us with all of creation. We repay this debt through faith and worship. The second debt is the debt we owe to the rshis for the wisdom they have given us. This debt is repaid through studying and sharing wisdom with others. Next, we owe a debt to our ancestors as they are the cause of our own birth. We thank them by acting in ways that show respect for our lineage and family.

The Shatpath Brahman adds two more debts. The first is a debt to humanity at large and we repay it by treating others with respect and dignity. Finally, we are indebted to nature and the plants and animals which provide us with life. We repay this debt by practicing good land stewardship and resource management.

Many people believe that they have difficulty in manifesting Artha related things such as food, clothing, shelter, work, etc… Usually the actual problem is that we are so afraid we will have difficulties in the future that we hold tightly onto everything we have, thus not practicing the Law of Circulation. If the idea is to give what we get, yet we aren't giving, then we are unlikely to get much either. So this is the first guideline to increasing our Artha.

Think about something in your life that you have always manifested easily. You can begin with something small; let's use books for an example. I have always manifested books easily; you can see that at my house. I have lots of books and I enjoy reading, learning new things, and sharing what I've learned through writing. If I examine my beliefs about books I can report that I am excited about them, I love the way they smell, how it feels to sit and read, how enjoyable it is to learn new things, and how much knowledge is available to me. I can truly experience this as being unlimited and easily available.

The next piece to this exercise is to take that experience of excitement, comfort, and unlimited availability and deepen it until I feel it surrounding and permeating my thoughts and senses. Allow yourself to do this with an example from your life. Really feel it! Once you've done that and can hold onto the experience allow your mind to consider an area of your life where you feel your powers of manifestation are not as well developed. Allow your feelings of unlimited availability to find a foothold there. Feel the power of your ability to manifest your desires in that area. Imagine yourself easily achieving your goals and creating all that you are seeking, and all that is seeking you.

The chakras of Artha include the third chakra, as it is our will and desire to manifest fully all that we require in life. The fourth chakra also keeps our activities in the realm of heart centered appreciation and gratitude for all that we have. We might even consider the fifth chakra, for the ability to communicate our goals, needs, and desires will also serve us in manifesting this goal.

mental

In this discussion of Artha it is important to remember that what we believe we will find in life is what we will create and discover. Life always demonstrates what is in our consciousness. If you expect life to always present you with good then good will show up all around you. On the other hand, if you expect that you will find not good, then life will meet that expectation as well.

The Arthashastra was written sometime around the 2nd to 4th century b.c. by Kautilya. This ancient scripture is a treatise on economics and statehood. One of the definitions of Arthashastra is *The Science of Material Gain*. As in other scriptures we can easily generalize many of the teachings to our own lives and circumstances. Lust, anger, greed, vanity, haughtiness, gluttony, envy, attachment, and sloth are all common qualities that are considered to be the gateways of hell on earth. Overcoming these conditions brings peace on earth, restrains the senses, and allows us to acquire wisdom through the company of our elders. With our senses under control we will maintain our *sadhana* – spiritual practice, avoid hurting others, and bring wealth and abundance into our kingdoms by avoiding "unrighteous and uneconomical" transactions.

According to Kautilya and the Arthashastra, wealth is the most important of the four goals for it allows us to pursue the others. Wealth allows us to find knowledge.

Consider our current era. Without some degree of wealth our educational opportunities may be limited because we can't afford to attend a university or forgo working in order to attend. With our educational choices limited, what we might do for work is also limited, as well as where we will live and how able we are to care for our families and other responsibilities.

Lack of Artha is a cause of suffering in the world for two reasons. The first is that without wealth we may be unable to meet basic needs, thus causing our health and wellbeing to suffer. The second is that the perception of lack increases our attachment and desire, leading us to addiction, unhappiness, greed, and envy. We cannot be happy and find peace of mind if we are suffering in this way. When we believe we do not have enough it is extremely difficult to see where we can give.

One of the most important practices when it comes to fulfilling our goal of Artha is to walk our talk. This means that we do what we say we are going to do, and act in accordance with what we profess to believe. Not doing so creates a discrepancy in our lives that is not wealth promoting. I know of a man who says he doesn't believe that people should be in the country illegally, yet when he needs to hire someone to provide inexpensive labor he hires illegal immigrants to do the job. Others complain about manufacturing jobs being outsourced to other countries with cheaper labor, then shop for everything at big box stores where the items were made in other countries with questionable labor practices.

It is important to vote with your dollars for economic health. Spend your money at businesses that support what is important to you, and live your life as if it is important. Create a life of integrity where your actions and choices are in alignment with your beliefs and values. These are the ideals important to the fulfillment of Artha.

Align yourself with wisdom. In the Hindu pantheon of Gods & Goddesses the Goddess of Wisdom is Saraswati, while the Goddess of Wealth is Laksmi. As Swamiji reminds us, if we worship only Laksmi she will come but won't stay long. However, praying to Saraswati will bring us wisdom, and She will be always be accompanied by Her Sister Laksmi. Wisdom is an extremely valuable resource as it allows us to understand where our True Wealth is. Our wealth has no value unless it is used, spent, or given away. The harder you work to keep it, the less happy it will make you. The souls residing within our resources require that they be used as they are meant to be. Cars want to be driven, brooms want to sweep, musical instruments want to be played, and money is for circulating and spending.

As in all else, the best use of resources involves making the world a better place. When needs are met, and attachments silenced, we will realize that our Artha can be used for a bigger purpose than simply gratifying personal needs and desires. As our understanding of wealth expands we begin to see that we are merely a conduit through which this particular form of Divine Energy flows; that God hasn't provided wealth to us to hoard but in order that we might share it with others; thus supporting the life we are interconnected with. It benefits oneself and the world to share with others according to the value they provide to us. If you are a part of a community that is of value, share with them. If you enjoy the art and music of others, support them. If God has blessed you, do the same and bless others.

spiritual

On a spiritual level Artha is what we offer to God, and the expression of our attainment of divinity. Unfortunately, we may believe that Artha is evidence of the strength of our devotion. If we are "good enough" then God will bless us with abundance and all that we desire. This belief leads us to the opposite belief as well – that those who are impoverished, or lacking in some other manner, must somehow "deserve" it, thus justifying keeping our wealth to ourselves.

While our desires must, and will, be met in this lifetime, or another, we can sometimes become confused as to what is an appropriate desire. We become attached to life turning out how we think it should be and every time we experience the absence of our desired outcome we think God has turned His back on us.

In the Devi Mahatmyam (The Glory of the Goddess) also known as the Chandi Path, we learn a method of overcoming the maya and moha we are caught up in. We are attached to so many things, and because we desire immortality more than anything, we find ourselves in defense of the Ego, clinging to relationships that don't serve us, engaging in unhealthy practices, and committing violence in our thoughts, words, and actions. We have forgotten who we are and the Great Ego has surely taken over our consciousness, if not the entire universe!

At the beginning of our story a King, named Good Thoughts, has been defeated in battle by the Destroyers of Worship. These enemies have taken over the kingdom itself and Good Thoughts is forced to flee into the forest. He soon arrives at the hermitage of the Intellect of Love where all live in peace. While happy there, after awhile the King begins to fret over what has happened, and all that he believes he no longer has, and so he resumes his suffering.

Soon, he meets a businessman named Pure Intuitive Perception who has also been cast out of his home by his greedy wife and children. He too had begun to fret over past events and so they go together to ask the Intellect of Love why it is that even though they have been cast out of their homes, their minds are still attached to their loved ones, and why can't they simply be happy where they are now instead of remaining attached to the ignorance and egotism of their past.

The rshi begins to teach them that Mahamaya – the Great Illusion, is the cause of all circumstances and relationships. She (the Goddess Durga) attracts us all to Her with such force that we become confused into believing that She is somehow separate from us. The force of our attraction causes us to believe that there is something beyond ourselves to attain. She is both the cause of our existence as well as our liberation from suffering.

The rshi goes on to tell them the story of how the Divine Mother came into being and how she defeats the armies of asuras (bad thoughts) that are seeking to destroy us. She begins by destroying the thoughts Too Much and Too Little before going on to engage in battle with the Great Ego and his armies. She slays Devoid of Clear Understanding, Fickleness, Haughtiness, Arrogance, Memories, Anxiety, Violent Temper, passion, the Great Deceiver, Hypocracy, Irresistible Temptations, Foulmouth, and many others until finally She destroys Self Conceit and Self Deprecation, the biggest trouble makers of all!

After this battle, all the people of the four worlds are happy and sing songs of praise and gratitude to the Goddess Chandi – She who Tears Apart Thought. In return She offers us the boon that whoever shall recite this story, with focused concentration, will have all of their difficulties slain by Her. They will never be troubled by bad things happening to them, they will never be separated from their loved ones; they will have no reason to fear from enemies or natural disasters. They will be blessed with health, wealth, and wisdom.

So, this Goddess has manifested to release us from our suffering on all levels and She then promises to continue to help us whenever we call upon Her. But isn't that the tricky part? When we need Her the most is when we forget that we already ARE Her! This is the true lesson of Artha. It is our belief that we are separate which causes us to experience the lack, but by simply remembering our relationship with the Divine and participating in our lives we allow our Bhakti (devotion) to bring us to the realization that everything we need is available now, and always will be. The meditation of the Chandi is that all of these battles are occurring within us. It isn't so much what the Divine Mother does for us, but the realization that we have within us the capacity to eradicate the asuras *because* She resides within, freeing us from our suffering simply by our remembrance of Her.

Laksmi is the Goddess of True Wealth. The word laksha indicates what it is that we are aiming for. Therefore, Laksmi is our goal. It's helpful for us to allow the meaning of **True Wealth** to expand and include all of our goals such as satisfaction in our personal relationships, our ability to love what we have and have what we want, and an understanding that to be fulfilled includes spiritual fulfillment. If we have these things we will certainly have achieved True Wealth, regardless of the size of our bank accounts.

It is said that there are Six Wealth's available to us and worthy of our pursuit. We all naturally possess the capacity for the attainment of the Six Wealth's. While they are certainly ours already, they are also life qualities that may require some effort to develop fully.

The first of these is Shama or equanimity. This implies that we manage control over our mind. We maintain an evenness of attitude even while under stress.

When we have equanimity we are calm and composed and we are able to maintain our composure whether we are experiencing our desires or our sorrows. Understanding that life is happening equally in the difficulties as it is in the pleasures allows us to be at peace regardless of what arises in life. Shama gives us the ability to focus our attention where we want it and maintain tranquility of mind.

The second Wealth is Dama, control of the senses so that they are not in control of us. In the Katha Upanishad there is an analogy which describes the intellect as the charioteer, the mind as the reins, and the horses as the sensory organs. If we don't keep control over our senses through the control of our mind then it doesn't matter how intelligent we are, we will be disorganized and unable to move in the direction we wish to go. Without the ability to restrain our senses we are unable to put our attention anywhere but on sensory gratification. We become addicted to this or that and are constantly chasing after temporary pleasures.

Uparati is the third Wealth. It is about keeping life simple and letting go of the things that keep us from our goal. With this wealth we are able to love ourselves and treat our lives with respect and care. We avoid doing things that will cause us difficulties and cheerfully accept whatever happens. This doesn't only imply letting go of physical items, but also our emotional and spiritual baggage. Letting go of that which we no longer require offers us the knowledge that we are already full and complete, we don't need "things" to make us so. We begin to separate ourselves from the ups and downs of worldly activity.

Next is Titiksha which we can think of as endurance or forbearance. This allows us to experience life without falling apart whenever some change in circumstance occurs. We accept everything that happens as a gift from God. After all... how are we to know in the moment whether something is good or bad? All of life is Prasad, God's gift to us, even when we are unable to see the good that is ours, it doesn't mean that our circumstances are not leading us directly to our goal. With this Wealth we are able to step aside and realize that everything changes; giving us the wisdom to be ok with the pairs of opposites that exist in the world, and the understanding to experience hardships with patience and compassion.

Fifth is sraddha, or faith. This includes faith in God, faith in the sacredness of life, and above all, faith in oneself. It is a willingness to know the unknown and stay firmly rooted on one's spiritual path with the faith that we are moving in the right direction. Sraddha is where faith and awareness meet, giving us the confidence to follow our hearts and our own intuitive wisdom.

Finally, our sixth Wealth is samadhana, being at ease with Life in general. From this Wealth we find ease and comfort in life regardless of the circumstances we are experiencing. This sense of peace results in greater concentration as we are no longer distracted by wants and disappointments.

The Six Wealth's teach us that Artha is all we truly possess. When we understand that we already have everything we could possibly require we will know our true worth and value.

Kama is the third goal in life and many people associate it with desire and sexual activity. While these certainly are aspects of Kama, in actuality Kama is *everything* that we might want or desire; which can include all sorts of things. Kama – *to desire,* includes Dharma – the desire *to do* what is ours to do, Artha – the desire *to have* what we want, and Moksha – the desire *to know* who we are. It is at the foundation of why we do anything in life, for without desire we often remain stuck in ignorance and apathy.

Looking at Kama from an inclusive perspective we understand it to include all that we want in life. We know of the association between Kama and sexual desire through the ancient text known as the *Kama Sutra*, and I will share insights on this scripture later in the Physical section of Kama, along with other ideas regarding relationship.

Kama includes all desire. We've come to believe that desire is bad and that wanting anything other than what we have in life will lead us to ruin. In fact, the Four Noble Truths of Buddhism teach us that it is only by relinquishing desire that we are able to overcome suffering. However, our problem isn't necessarily desire itself; it is an attachment to the outcome of our desire. If we allow desire to pass through our consciousness without clinging to it, simply noticing as it ebbs and flows, then those desires begin to have no more of a hold on us than any other thought.

Unrequited desire keeps us looped in this cycle of birth, death and rebirth. Our desires must be met, that is a principle within the laws of karma. A desire, by its very nature, implies that there must be fulfillment of it in some form; just as every action carries within it a requirement for a result. Reincarnation, the rebirth of the Soul into another physical form, is intimately connected to Kama. It is desire that keep us embodied, returning life after life. Attachment to the many desires that arise for the embodied soul stay with us past the death of our current physical form, and remain as an unexpressed need for fulfillment in the next body we inhabit. This is why we benefit by choosing to move beyond our attachments to whatever it is that we desire now. Desire keeps us wanting more, more, more! Whether those desires are pure, such as the desire for God, unity, and the good of our community; or impure, such as the desire for ego gratification or revenge – they are still desires, thus keeping us caught up in the cycle of birth, death, and rebirth.

Eventually we come to the realization that most of our desires are not going to lead us to our greatest good. We may even believe that we are not, for whatever reason, worthy of achieving our goals. When this happens we sublimate our desires, pushing them deep into the shadowy confines of our darkest mental closet. We hide them there with the hope that they will go away on their own. The problem with this theory, as every psychologist knows, is that whenever we push these desires into our shadowy depths they don't go away… instead, they creep around waiting for a crack in our carefully constructed armor; an opening that will allow them to jump out, wreaking havoc on our lives!

Consider the woman who embezzles money from her spiritual community, or the man who sexually molests his stepchild. Both of these people may be known for their good works in the world, and seen as upstanding community members; yet they obviously have deeply sublimated issues and desires that are playing out in their lives. If you were to think about your challenges in life by asking yourself "what is this here to teach me?" instead of "what did I do to deserve this?" you would begin to understand how desire wraps itself around and through your consciousness, manifesting with in all of the circumstances of your life.

The goal is to bring awareness to our desires. Why do we want this or that? How will it improve our lives? What will we achieve if we are able to attain it? Will it bring us closer to our Self?

Kama offers us an exploration into the opposites in life. It bridges the gap between have and have not and is always looking outside of itself for answers. As part of the bridge between Dharma and Moksha, Kama leads us to seek a life of greater experience and self-expression than that which we have previously known. But Kama is also that which keeps us separate. Its very nature insists that there is something outside of us, something to attain, something more than whom we are or what we have.

There is a verse (Ch.1 V.55-56) in the Devi Mahatmyam, also known as the Chandi Path as translated by Swami Satyananda Saraswati, which states:

jñānināmapi cetāṃsi devī bhagavatī hi sā balādākṛṣya mohāya mahāmāyā prayacchati

She, this Supreme Goddess, the Great Measurement of Consciousness, attracts the perceiving capacity of all sensible beings with such force as to thrust them into the ignorance of egotistic attachment.

This verse specifically teaches us that as long as we believe that Truth is outside of us, we will continue to desire. Whenever we want something, anything – even God, the more we cling to the idea of attainment, the further we find ourselves from our goal. This is one of the primary human paradoxes. How do we achieve yoga, or unity, when the stronger our desire for it is the further away from it we find ourselves?

Also within the realm of Kama lie our emotions and feelings. Things like personal satisfaction and sensory pleasures entangle us in maya. As we traverse the landscape of our Spiritual path we begin to become aware of the feelings of others, realizing that the rest of the world doesn't consider us to be the center of creation, it is only we ourselves who believe this. While it is normal to orient the conditions of the world in relationship to yourself, it is not appropriate to expect others to orient conditions to you as well. They have their own path to walk.

Lord Kama believes He has the power to distract even Lord Shiva from His meditations; it's no wonder that our own desires keep us from doing the things we know are in our best interest.

Perhaps desire is simply a part of our nature. Do we ever do anything that is free from desire? As physically embodied souls we are Beings of Desire. Understanding this allows us to begin noticing which desires we are choosing to cling to. Our desires can be extremely strong and compelling; for most of us our task lies in learning to desire in appropriate ways.

If we turn our dreams towards our True Purpose - realization of the Self, we find that there are many ways to express Bhakti, or devotion. Devotion and desire are, in fact, two sides of the same coin. On the one hand we have desires which fiercely attract us to that which we perceive to be separate from us; and, on the other, we have devotion which creates within us the heart space to simply love and be at one with the Indwelling Spirit. Both desire and devotion require seeking something, yet devotion is an acknowledgement that we already have some piece within us of that which we desire. Ultimately, it is impossible to have one without the other. The goal is that we learn to find such perfect balance that we move beyond this cosmic embrace of Shiva/Shakti and into the Pure Essential Beingness that is All, Everything, the Holy Whole Enchilada.

> *The Prophet said that Truth has declared: "I am not hidden in what is high or low, or in the earth nor skies nor throne. This is certainty, O beloved: I am hidden in the heart of the faithful. If you seek me, seek in these hearts."*
>
> *Jalaludin Rumi*

Rumi, the much loved 12th century Sufi poet teaches us that the way through our separation is through devotion, and into the very heart of love. For this is the Truth underlying all faith… we already are that which we seek. This is the lesson of Kama, that desire is nothing but seeking outside of ourselves for our Beloved.

One of the things that is important for us to keep in mind when seeking to manifest our desires is whether any specific desire is pure or impure. A pure desire is one born from the seeds of love. It will lead us to greater goodness, a stronger sense of community, and more love in the world. Impure desires are those which take away from others in order for us to gain. If I can see that my desire will hurt you or take away from another's joy in life, then I would do better to understand that that desire will never bear good fruit.

The houses of astrology that reflect our journey through the experience of Kama include the third, seventh, and the 11th. The third house signifies our siblings, friends, and other associations. It's easy to see how, through our relationships with the others in our lives, we contribute to our experiences of Kama. The seventh house is the house of our relationships with a significant other, or spouse. The 11th house indicates the gains that we hope to achieve through our work in the world.

physical

Kama on the physical level is about choice. What brings us to choose a behavior is influenced by many things, both internal and external. If our goal is to respond to these choices in ways which are full and complete expressions of our greatest good, we must plan ahead; or at least be able to conceptualize what the likely results of our actions will be.

Imagine how much easier your life would seem if you could "see" into the drama's and dharma's of your future. You could avoid that potential accident or disappointing relationship! The good news is that we *can* see into our future – at least up to a certain point. Our future life is a direct result of everything that has gone on before it... every choice, and every success or failure; all of it. If you want to see into the future consider what your actions of today might lead to, what karmic arrows you will release, or what choice was made in the past that brought you to your current state of affairs.

What do you desire most in the world? What do you want so badly that you are willing to experience great joy, as well as great sorrow? What brings you pleasure? What do you strive for? These are a few questions that might help you in unlocking the mysteries of Kama. Understanding these mysteries is a challenge for even the most adventurous of us. We may be attracted to a person, group, idea, or practice but are the results of attaining that goal something we are willing to live with?

In developing this goal regard familial and other relationships, in fact – consider all that you are in relationship with. The only way to do this is to stay present within your moment, attending to it and its possibilities and repercussions for the future. Without doing so you will become confused and unable to make appropriate choices for yourself or others.

When we think of physical desire our first thoughts often include sexuality and intimacy. The scriptures of the Kama Sutra by Vatsyayana, believed to have been written sometime in the 2nd century, although archaic, teach us about sexual relationships, along with the associated values and practices of those relationships. The Sutras describe for us the role of sexual pleasure in the life of a householder, generally considered to be a man who has completed his education and is now building his home and lifestyle, in great detail. The Sutras discuss how to acquire a wife and what to do with her once you have found her. They teach us how to approach the goals of Dharma, Artha, & Kama. This scripture describes for us the ways in which pleasure is found; that there are certain arts which women, in particular, should study and how they are to be treated. It is understood throughout this text that women are a valuable and pleasurable part of a man's life and that they should be treated with respect and integrity.

From the Kama Sutra we learn about more than sexuality, we also learn how to behave in public, and how to show respect towards others. We learn about all of our relationships, not just as lovers, but also how to be with our friends; and how those relationships might improve or diminish our social standing. As every teenager knows, sexual practices are discussed in great detail within the Kama Sutra; however, the sutras are certainly not limited to that topic.

What choices do you make regarding intimacy and sexuality? By today's standards the Kama Sutras are fairly tame; reading them one can only imagine how the minds of early Indians worked. We see that the community was strongly interconnected with home life, and how anything can be sacred with attention to detail and an understanding of how to behave within the guidelines of acceptable behavior and practices.

These ideas of appropriate behavior are very much a part of desire and pleasure. In order for the goal of Kama to be practiced we must keep in mind certain qualifications such as: is the pleasure consensual? Do you practice unsafe sex or choose to stay with an obviously wrong partner, even when you know that it could cost you your sanity, or your life? Is your desire so strong at times that nothing will stand in your way? While darker desires are aspects of Kama as well, we must be mindful that we are harming no-one by our choice of activities. Kama practices must ALWAYS be consensual. "No" & "stop" **always** mean "no" & "stop".

Keeping in mind that our ultimate pure desire is our desire for God, we begin to understand that all desires are leading us towards the truth that we cannot attain our goals by seeking outside of ourselves. All of the desires of life are intended to keep us pointing in that direction. We won't begin to approach the Divine so long as we are still caught up in the objects and relationships of the world.

Addiction is another part of the physical aspect of Kama. When we become addicted our entire body/mind becomes consumed with the desire to obtain and use our substance or behavior of choice. Even our brain structures change in response to these desires. Our bodies crave relief and all that we do will become an effort to obtain and use. In my classes, I define addiction as anything which alters our brain chemistry and that we continue to do despite negative consequences. Is there anything is your life that fits those criteria?

Most of us have a tendency to either focus strongly on the pursuit of pleasure, or the denial of it. We tend to practice either excess or abstinence, while neglecting the middle ground of moderation. Life is not an either/or state of affairs. Finding a middle ground allows us to satisfy Kama along with the other three goals.

The way to save ourselves from excessive indulgence, and find balance in the desire versus devotion continuum, is through moderation. Too little keeps us caught in the throes of searching and wanting, too much and we become dominated by our desires and ego.

As St. Paul said in 1 Corinthians 7:9 of the Bible "But if they cannot contain, let them marry: for it is better to marry than to burn." This reminds us that our desires are meant to be fulfilled and if we don't respond and satisfy them during this lifetime we will carry those seeds of desire into the next. It does not benefit us to suffer; our lives are not tests of endurance, they are classrooms for growth. If our desires are pure then we are meant to achieve and enjoy them, for it is through the practice of pleasure where we manifest more love and joy in the Life of God.

I once had a conversation with a friend about pure versus impure desire. A pure desire was defined as a desire that connects us to something larger than our personal experience such as a desire for community, or a desire for God. It connects us to others and we can define it as a practice. An impure desire is something we seek for selfish or egoic reasons… it becomes a habit where we are hoping to fulfill something that is only about ourselves. An impure desire doesn't involve a relationship whereas a pure desire is always a relationship strengthening drive.

The Chakra of Desire is the second – the Svadhistana. The color of this chakra is orange. Essential oils, aphrodisiacs, massage, and stimulants directly affect this chakra by stimulating and/or moderating excessive desire. Our fourth chakra – the Anahata, with the color green is also influenced by our desires. The fire of our devotion burns away the impurities, lifting our desire up into that higher, heart-centered chakra.

mental

How does Kama impact us on a mental level? To begin with, we might ask ourselves what it is that we really want. Clarity regarding our desires allows us to create an efficient plan of action for the achievement of our goals. So often we catch ourselves spinning around in circles hoping to attain something only to realize that this *thing* is no longer important to us. Or, we obtain it only to realize that it wasn't what we had hoped it would be, and that the cost far outweighed the benefits. We are so inundated with hopes and dreams to achieve that we often find ourselves infatuated with the latest gizmo only to realize as soon as we get it that something newer and shinier has caught our attention.

Cheating in a relationship is similar "grass is greener" thinking. I recently read a study titled 'Why Men Cheat.' The researcher determined that cheating is a result of the man feeling that his needs are not being met in the relationship. I believe that this study applies equally to both men and women, but I see two problems with this theory. First, the cheating partner may or may not have let the partner know what their needs are. Many times in relationship we expect our significant others to be mind readers – "if he/she really loved me they would know what I need." Unfortunately, most of us have enough trouble knowing what it is in our own minds that we want, let alone have the ability to accurately determine what is on someone else's mind.

The second problem is that when we cheat on someone it is really unreasonable to blame them for our behavior. As adults we have choices, and Kama is really about making appropriate choices regarding our desires and how we shall go about achieving them. Blaming others for our bad behavior is simply an excuse so that we can avoid taking on the responsibility of acting like an adult. No-one else is responsible for our behavior. No-one makes us act in a certain way, feel feelings we don't accept, or believe in anything that we don't agree to.

If you were to honestly take a look back at your past relationships you would likely notice that they were all with the same person, except they were wearing different bodies. The problem isn't your partner. Remember that the common denominator in all of your relationships is yourself. Until you are able to look at your own input and impact on the relationship you are likely to keep finding the same person over and over again. Your justifications and excuses prevent you from ever honestly seeing yourself or your partner in the relationship. It is rarely helpful to spend time thinking about how the others in your life have done you wrong. It is always beneficial to consider what your part in the problem was, or is.

Almost always we hurt ourselves more than anyone else ever could as a result of our actions and choices.

Inadvertent or not, if we don't think ahead and consider the ramifications of what we do today we will shoot karmic arrows off into many experiences and lifetimes to come. While this certainly doesn't apply only to our relationships, when we are acting in unacceptable and unproductive ways our most direct feedback comes to us as a result of the light of understanding found through the gaze of our most intimate others.

When you think of pleasure… where does your mind go? Do you think of things that will ultimately be the cause of more harm and suffering than good? Where is the pleasure in that? These desires will only amount to a momentary change in your state of consciousness. Real pleasure is seeking that which will offer you a permanent change for the better. You will never find that outside of yourself.

What are some of the reasons people don't feel pleasure? Pleasure is one of those experiences that we choose. Just as anger and happiness are emotional choices we make, so is pleasure. We decide for ourselves in each moment what our experience of life is to be. Some people don't believe they deserve pleasure; that for some real or imagined transgression, which they may or may not have been responsible for, they are being punished and kept from the Promised Land of Redemption and Joy in Life.

We have incarnated in these times, with the families we have chosen, to experience life, fulfill our karmic obligations, and come to the realization that life is now, and has always been, uniquely perfect. The life we have is to our exact specifications based upon our thoughts, beliefs, and actions. Knowing that of all the possible families to have been born into I chose mine can be an amazing revealer of who I am and what my lessons for this lifetime are, if I allow myself to see the truth. Our ancestors also played a guiding part in leading each of us into this moment of our existence through their experiences, not to mention the choices we personally have made.

One extremely effective way to calm our mind when we are finding it difficult to find moderation in our desires is through the practice of japa or mantra yoga. Japa is the repetition of a word or phrase for a specified number of times or amount of time. I find that it is better to choose a phrase that is affirming the state of mind we want to foster, rather than saying what we don't want. For example: if we are challenged by thoughts of anger we might choose to say something like "I accept the circumstances of my life and learn from them." Or, if we are lusting after a person or substance we say "I am whole and complete, right now and just as I am."

One affirmation that is generally helpful is "There is One Life, that Life is God's Life. That Life is perfect. That life is my Life now." Or perhaps try chanting Om Namah Sivaya. Feel free to choose any affirmative phrase or word that you find to be helpful for you.

One of the most important spiritual teachers we have had is Sri Ramana Maharshi. One thing he taught us is that ritual, mantra, and meditation are the three primary practices for achieving God-Realization. Ritual includes worship and seva, as well as those practices that assist us in maintaining the health of our physical body such as yoga and ayurveda.

Mantra purifies our speech and calms our mind. Our words have power because as we speak the tip of our tongue, which corresponds to the Saraswati nadi, is stimulated by touching upon various areas within our mouths. The nadis can be thought of as the energetic nervous system which connects our subtle body to our physical body. As we speak and our tongue activates these energy points our words transition from being simple sounds, to having the ability to create our experiences. If we tend to talk in the negative, or gossip, or say things that are untrue, mean or hateful we will program our subtle body to create those experiences in our life. On the other hand, by being mindful of our speech, chanting divine words and names, and speaking in cheerful, honest and helpful ways we open up our creativity to the creation of good for ourselves and the world.

From our practice of mantra we are able to move more easily into meditation, for then we will have found a purity of Spirit that will allow us to move beyond desire and into the Realization of our own Divine Perfection.

spiritual

Kama is the practice of relationship. There is nothing we desire more than to achieve Oneness with our Beloved. Just as we need a mirror in order to see our physical reflection we need relationships to know who we are. The faces of our companions in life are the mirrors which validate us and bring understanding to our personal experience of who we are in the world. We are the manifestation of all divinity and the representation of God within our individualized expression of life.

Although we might want to believe differently, we are animals requiring physical contact and acceptance. Living in human bodies allows us the ultimate opportunity to experience, express, and explore sensual pleasures along with the consciousness that allows us to seek out a relationship with the Divine. If our senses were unimportant we wouldn't need bodies to attain God. It isn't attaining, or even having, a desire that keeps us bound in suffering, it is holding onto our attachment regarding the outcome of that desire. It is only by either fulfilling our desires or releasing them that we find freedom from them, but if we believe that the attainment of them is the source of our happiness we are attached and will remain bound.

As Mark Epstein writes in his book *Open to Desire*, "it's not desire that is the problem; it's that your desires are too small." What this implies is that we often keep our attention on the common, day to day desires, when we should be setting our gaze on more expansive goals. We want to keep our attention broad in order that we are able to see the most complete picture of the likely outcomes of our choices. If we are seeking all that comes to mind in order to satisfy our moment to moment quirks and queries, we soon become caught up in the mundane desires of physical embodiment, completely missing God sitting in front of us placing the world in our hands.

The very soul of Kama is devotion – Bhakti. Devotion is desire's most pure form. The meaning of Love is to take your desire and transform it into an act of worship. Unless you look upon your beloved as if you were seeing the Divine incarnate, you cannot achieve the love your soul desires. This isn't about finding love, it is about *being* love. Love is what we *do*, it is a verb not a noun, and it requires action.

It is in the open-hearted playground of bhakti where we find our fullest expression of Kama. Devotion is the dance of Shiva and Shakti, consciousness and bliss. This Divine Embrace is the desire/devotion continuum and Tantra is the practice of worshipping our Beloved in all of Her forms. Ishvara Pranidhana is bowing down in devotion to God. This devotion asks us to surrender our lives to the Greater Life that is around us, requiring that we "lean into" whatever experience comes to us.

We have many examples of this love. Think of Krishna – the Lord of Love, and Radhe, his companion in the Gardens of Vrindavan. Or Sita and Rama, the Divine Couple residing in the heart of Sri Hanuman. To prove his devotion Hanuman jumped over the Ocean and burned Lanka to the ground in order to reunite those lovers.

To do this requires faith, or sraddha. A helpful practice in assisting us along the path towards the realization that God is All There Is, for some, may be to practice chanting and studying the meaning of the Tantroktam Devi Suktam from the Chandi Path. These verses remind us that the Divine Goddess is in all existence, manifesting as intelligence, sleep, hunger, appearance, energy, forgiveness, humility, peace, faith, beauty, wealth, activity, recollection, compassion, confusion, as the form of Mother, and pervading over all beings and through all existence. When we can recognize God in all forms we begin to see Her movements through our own lives, minds, and hearts.

The key is to understand that these are all qualities to be found within us; and that we will never find them outside of our Selves. The practice of Vedic Tantra teaches us to be mindful and conscious in all that we do. Paying attention to our work in the world creates a life of compassion and efficiency. It teaches us to clean up the karmic messes we might otherwise be tempted to sweep under the rug; a short term fix that puts it all off until another day.

As we worship and perform Puja we learn to recognize that because God is all there is, any given quality of God can be found within our own hearts. We create a relationship with our Beloved and use this divine union to improve all of the other relationships which we have created – for they are all this One Holy Embrace. In fact, the closer you can come to embracing all of the activities and circumstances of your life, the nearer you will find the Divine Mother. When you can hold your life in pure, sacred love, accepting all that is, you will certainly find yourself seated firmly in Her lap.

This doesn't mean to imply that everything in your life from then on will always meet your hopes and expectations. You will still have karma to unfold and fulfill. The goal is to learn to reduce the karma you create. One way to do this is through the practice of Bramacharya. Bramacharya can be translated as "walking with God." In this practice we live as if God is walking beside us at all times. How do you behave when all you see is God? What if your nosy neighbor, beloved niece, forgetful parent, stranger at the grocery store – were God? What if the billions of people starving right now, as you read this, are God? Or the Earth Herself – Bhu Devi; what if she were God?

It may be an easy task to think of our loved one, perhaps even certain strangers, as Divine, but what about people who do despicable, horrible, heart-wrenching acts? Can we find God in those individuals? For if God is everywhere She must be there as well. Our lesson here may be to learn about the "new F–word" as a popular youtube video portrays. This video shows a minister during his sermon telling us about the "new f-word" in church. The word is to *forgive*. He then encourages the congregation to turn to their neighbors and say "F – you!" To go home and say F – you to their families, to say F – you to their bosses, maybe even stand on a rooftop and yell "F- all y'all"!!!

In the practice of Bramacharya we practice moderation in all that we do. Remember though, we may each have different ideas regarding what is moderation and what is excess. It is important that we live by the vows we have made and to organize our lives in ways that allow us to live in integrity, ethically and truthfully. Just as we generally think of Kama as being about sex, we also may believe that to practice Bramacharya means that we practice celibacy. If we take a vow of celibacy then we would certainly want to honor that. If we don't take such a vow, we might instead avoid random sex, unsafe sex, or illegal sex. The point here is that when we develop the boundaries of our behavior, and make appropriate choices in our daily adventures, we are still walking with God.

Remember though, Bramacharya isn't only about sexual behavior. To walk with God implies that we are mindful and considerate in all that we do. We consider where our food comes from and the suffering its manufacture has created in the world; we make choices regarding where we spend our resources and the activities we support through those resources; we learn to stop when we have had enough, rather than to continue on past the satisfaction of our desires and into the indulgences of our addictions.

Kama comes to us spiritually through the development of ojas. Ojas is the nectar distilled from that which we have consumed. As we take in nourishment from the world outside of us and it goes through the various systems of our bodies it becomes transformed by the metabolic fire of Agni. All waste products are burned away or carried out of the body and what is left is a milky substance that connects the physical being with consciousness. Ojas is the basis for the feeling of love. Just as a mother nourishes her child with the milk from her breasts, our Divine Mother nourishes us with the milky ojas produced from love. The higher vibration of the food we eat, and the love we express, the purer and sweeter the ojas we produce. Bring to mind a time when your heart was filled with love and remember the feeling of that sweet nectar pouring through every cell of your being so strongly that you were able to feel it as it flowed out to all around you.

Once I had the blessing of participating in a kirtan performance that lasted for several hours. When we finished, and as we were taking down the altar and clearing off the stage, I spoke with a man who had been playing with us. Both of our hearts were so open that after chatting a bit we hugged and breathed together for a few moments. We could feel our hearts open and the ojas flowing between us. The ojas created from hours of devotional practice was beautifully overwhelming and thoughts of him arise in my mind whenever I think of that day.

As we develop ojas we find that our lives become infused with love and this love spills out, pouring into all that we do, think, and become. It is the essence of tantra, and of Kama.

moksha

The fourth goal in life is Moksha, and it is our ultimate goal in life. Moksha is the process of rediscovering the truth of our being in a physical body and returning to a remembrance of the Self. By this I mean the Self with a capital "S", the Self that is ever present, never changing, in all places, all the time. It is this goal of transcendence that carries us through the world of objects and their relationships and into an understanding that there is only one of us here; one Self, one Life, one Existence.

Moksha is our relationship to Truth and Reality. It lifts us above our limitations, beliefs, desires, and attachments, allowing us the experience of pure consciousness, unity & yoga. If you have ever experienced being a *witness* to your life then you have experienced a taste of this transcendence. If you have ever felt yourself to be fully present in the current moment, you have seen a glimpse of Reality.

We often think of Moksha as *enlightenment* but how would we define that so as to know when we are having the experience? Wikipedia defines it as "a final blessed state free from ignorance, desire and suffering." Since these states (ignorance, desire, and suffering) are all transient then Moksha must refer to a state where we are no longer influenced by maya and moha. Is it even possible to achieve Moksha while still a jiva, or embodied soul?

Some would say "no, it wouldn't be possible." Human existence is characterized by ignorance –the belief that we are separate from God; desire – believing that there is something outside of ourselves that we must be constantly reaching for; and suffering – the fruit of our attachments to these desires and beliefs. Due to these characteristics of life in a body we are easily and constantly becoming entangled in webs of deception. However, reality and truth inform us that we are, in fact, eternal souls having human experiences. Thus, Moksha isn't a goal to reach for from the understanding of our human life, but a realization from the standpoint of our Infinite Self. So while jiva we can gain an understanding of Moksha because it is the nature of a Reality from which we are never separate.

Moksha isn't a goal to attain; it is a Reality to remember! When we remember, we find liberation from our attachment to the objects and relationships of human existence. When we remember, we realize that we are not subject to the passage of time and space. When we remember, we recognize the integrity of our Wholeness. As Gerald May wrote: "God is closer to us, the mystics say, than our breath; closer than we are to ourselves." St. John of the Cross said, "We are in God like a stone is in the earth ... already in the Center." There is no way to get any closer to God than we already are. The spiritual life is not about actually coming closer to God but rather the realization of a communion and unity that already exists, always has, and always will... forever.

We begin our journey of this goal when we ask ourselves "what is the meaning of life?" However, we usually understand this question as "what is its meaning for me, right now and in this moment?" The difference between these two questions is that the first keeps us separate because to ask a philosophical question such as that implies duality. We know the truth of this because we all have a different response intended to answer this question globally, and in the same way for everyone. When we inquire into philosophy we have begun to seek outside of ourselves. If instead, we ask the second question, we must turn within for the answer. Self-inquiry means that the answer cannot be found by looking anywhere but inward. The answer to this question is different for everyone.

As humans we have an inner drive to find transcendence, but we are short on attention. While some of us are able to maintain a long term spiritual discipline, most of us go from one tradition, religion, spiritual teacher, or philosophy to another. Attempting to find God in this manner is like trying to find water by digging small shallow holes. The only way to properly dig a well is to dig deeply in one place. If we want to attain Moksha we must be willing to dig one deep hole. Making a commitment to a Guru is like digging a well. The word Guru literally means – One who removes the darkness (of our spiritual ignorance). By paying attention not only to the Guru's teaching but also to how they live their life, and by doing our best to emulate them, will assist us along our path as we eradicate our separation and learn to live efficiently and in integrity.

The astrological houses of Moksha include the fourth, the eighth, and the 12th. The fourth house is our house of home, where we belong. From the perspective of Moksha this house indicates that it is a sense of belonging that resides within our hearts and leads us to Moksha. The eighth house is the house of death, endings, and transitions. It teaches us to move beyond the objects and relationships of our lives. The 12th house, the last of the zodiac, is the final barrier we pass through before beginning, once again, our journey through the cycle of birth, death and rebirth.

physical

Achieving Moksha from a physical perspective requires that we transcend the limitations of being in a body. If we are prone to noticing limitation in our life we may believe that we are blocked in our transpersonal growth by the limiting appearances of poverty, disease or upbringing. In reality, simply setting appropriate goals for ourselves is what will set us free from our perceived limitations. We know the truth of this when we see an amputee climb a mountain, or a child learn to accomplish a new skill.

Attempting to go through our lives without setting goals is like trying to drive from San Francisco to Chicago without a map. I know that I have used this metaphor previously, but it applies here as well. Eventually we may, by chance, arrive in Chicago, but if we do it will be due to pure good fortune. More likely, we will drive around aimlessly, become sidetracked on interesting detours, or find ourselves suddenly waking up to realize that we have been hypnotized by the siren's call after having spent days, months, or years lost in a dream we neither wanted nor expected! If only we had set goals for ourselves and looked for the ducks and candles that would show us we are on the right trail.

This is really what setting a goal requires. Imagining where you want to be at some point in the future is your first step. Deciding how you will get from where you are now to where you hope to be and then, of course, knowing how to recognize that you have arrived once you are there. Can you imagine the possibilities you will find by approaching life in this way?

For many people transcendence requires overcoming addictions and habits that keep them stuck in their current experience. What is it about addiction that keeps us doing the same thing over and over again? When we are under the spell of an addiction, we're in the process of changing our brains, and its neurochemical responses, essentially hard-wiring ourselves, to repeat the behavior, over and over again.

As humans we are hardwired to alter our consciousness. Since the beginning of time, when we first discovered certain plants that have the ability to change our perceptions, or we discovered that allowing grains to ferment in a wet basket would create a mind altering beverage, humankind has been using these substances in an attempt to expand into the unknown. Unfortunately, many of these substances interfere with neurochemical responses in the brain, changing our natural ability to reconnect with our own Divine nature. In our attempt to liberate ourselves from our common everyday experiences we have forgotten that we have the ability within ourselves, through the practice of meditation, to know and realize that we are already situated firmly in the state we are seeking.

Neti, neti is a Sanskrit phrase meaning *not this, not that*. If in our meditation practice we focus our attention on the question "who am I?" and upon each answer remind ourselves that we are not this or that, not our name, not our physical appearance, not our job, not the roles that we engage in, not what other people think of us, not even what we think of ourselves; and that all of the illusions which seem to separate us from God, are merely illusions we will begin to understand our True Nature. When with each answer we offer ourselves we respond neti, neti, we begin to move inward towards that flame of knowing within our hridaya, the spiritual heart, which offers us the truth of our being.

In this way we transcend the limitations of being in a body, for our physical forms are truly limitations and hindrances on our spiritual journey to Moksha. How much easier life would be if it weren't for being in a body! Meditating on that reminds us that we are beyond this illusion of creation; that we are, in fact, unlimited beings experiencing the illusion of limitation. We are here as spiritual beings having a human experience. This human experience allows us to satisfy our karma, create new karma, learn to be in relationship, and grow in whatever ways aren't possible while unembodied.

What does it mean to be enlightened while in a physical body? It is finding balance between caring for our body as a vehicle for our soul, while at the same time maintaining an attitude of being in the world but not of the world. It requires making choices which will lead us toward our goal of liberation, rather than choices which will carve ever deeper samskaras into our consciousness. Enlightenment in the physical body implies that we recognize ourselves as part of a larger system, understanding that we are not separate from the world we live in.

Once, while I was on an extended trip into the wilderness, I was hiking upon a trail when I came upon a tree that had been struck by lightning at some point in its history. This hollow and burned-out tree had a hole in it at just the right height for me to put my head into. For some reason I was compelled to do that, and as I stood there with my head in this tree breathing in the scent of the earth, the dampness, and the smell of burnt wood, I suddenly experienced an overwhelming sense of love. The thought entered my mind that even though we humans engage in all sorts of activities that serve to separate ourselves from the Earth, we are Her children anyway. Just as any good mother loves her children unconditionally, Bhu Devi, Mother Earth, loves us in that same unconditional and eternal way.

This realization brought me to tears. Earlier that day I had looked out over a part of the forest that had been clear-cut, had noticed chemical trails in the sky, walked past an area where the ruins lay of an old, abandoned mine still showed a deep gash in the landscape, and I'd been thinking of all the ways in which humans have impacted the integrity of the earth. Now this understanding that She loves us anyway, regardless of what we do, perhaps even in spite of what we do, helped me in the understanding that there is so much more here than I can comprehend. I came to the realization, that despite appearances, there is only one of us here. While we act in ways that are reprehensible, destructive, and that take no other life into account, we are only hurting ourselves.

Our subtle body, and the seat of our consciousness, is made up of five sheaths or koshas. The first of these is the Annamaya Kosha. This is the sheath made up of food, it is our physical body. The second kosha is the Pranamaya kosha and is created from our breath, prana. Next, the Manomaya kosha is the realm of the mind. The fourth kosha is the Jnanamaya kosha, the realm of wisdom. Finally, we have the Anandamaya kosha, our bliss body; that part of ourselves that is divine and always connected to God. The more of our time and energy we devote to the outer koshas, the deeper our connection to Source. Placing our energy on the inner koshas, our food and breath bodies, limits our attention to that which is temporary.

The chakras of Moksha include the sixth, the Ajna chakra, located near the pineal gland, in the center of the head behind the eyebrows, and the Sahasrara chakra located at the top of the head. These chakras connect our, physical body, and our subtle body, with our intuitive perception, and allow for direct connection with Brahma.

mental

Sometime during the third century B.C.E. a philosopher named Plato gave us a famous allegory, or teaching story, which still applies today. He explained to us that if a group of people were kept shackled in a cave where all they could see were the shadowy images upon a back wall, that everything they would believe in, and the only experience they would know, would be that of illusion and of dancing shadows. The people of the cave would believe life was simply the interplay of smoke and shadow and existed without real substance or form. Because there had been nothing else in their experience these people, regardless of what anybody might tell them, would believe that the images on the wall were the truth of all there is.

Plato goes on to tell us how, if someone were taken from the cave and brought out into the light of day, they would be so blinded by the light that it would be impossible for them to believe that what they saw was real. As their pupils contracted against the glare, and their mind rebelled against this new information and vision of the world, it is likely that they would believe they had gone mad. And in fact, when they were returned to the cave, that place of illusion and captivity, their friends in the cave would also believe that they had gone out into the sun, their eyes had burnt, and they had lost their minds.

Even in our present time, when faced with ideas or beliefs that are contrary to our fixed and limited notions, we often resist what is new or that has not been a part of our previous experience. Many of us resist new ideas, feeling more comfortable with what we already know, even if those old structures are no longer working or appropriate. We are unwilling, or perhaps unable, to move on into a new paradigm of thought or activity. We might even believe that something is true just because somebody told us that it is, without ever seeking to find out for ourselves, or even questioning whether what we have been taught aligns with our own perception of truth.

We are often attached to our current reality for it is much easier, and often more comfortable, to continue playing hide and seek with the demons we know; even if we know that those demons are causing us great pain and suffering. To take the risk and step out into a world of the unknown, where new dragons might be lurking around the corner, requires more fortitude than someone who has spent their life in a cave might be able to muster up. But this is exactly what it takes to move into conscious liberation. We must be willing to transcend the beliefs we agreed to live by before we knew the repercussions of those ideas.

True freedom comes from knowing our limitations. If you were put into a completely dark room in which you had never been before, you would not be free. Any movement might cause you to trip over a chair or run into the wall. The only way you would find freedom there would be to turn on a light; for the light will show you where the limitations are, and light is what leads us to our transcendence. The light makes us free. It allows us to plan our lives; and it allows us to wake up. Just as physical Moksha involved transcending the limitations of being in a body, mental Moksha requires transcending the beliefs that have kept us limited.

This mental Moksha requires that we experience and experiment with new ideas by taking them into the cave of our own hearts, meditating upon them, and finding the truth for ourselves. How do we accomplish this? Part of growing up means that we become willing to learn new things, and allow ourselves to entertain the possibilities that are all around us; far too often we have allowed our fears and attachment to keep us from stepping out of the cave and into the light.

Jyotish, Vedic astrology, offers us a way to understand our minds, as well as our place in the cosmology of our lives. Jyotish might be thought of as a map of the cosmos as it appeared at the moment of our birth. It contains the influences affecting our experience of this lifetime. In fact, the word Jyotish means *light on life*. Our charts, just as shining a light in a dark room offers us freedom, offer us the freedom that enlightenment brings. Jyotish assists us in planning our lives by pointing out the karma we have come into this body with, possible events for our time here, and provides instruction on how to navigate the deep waters and slippery slopes of physical embodiment.

Waking up is the best, and most important, thing we can do for ourselves, now or during any other moment in time. The problem is that most of us don't know we are asleep, the dream has captured us and we've remained in the darkness of our spiritual ignorance. But when any one of us is brave enough to venture out of the cave, open our eyes in the sunlight and entertain the possibility of an expanding consciousness, our collective consciousness experiences even greater potential for awakening.

A bodhisattva is someone who has committed to the cycle of birth, death, and rebirth until all sentient beings have become enlightened. These great souls continue to remind us that we don't have to remain asleep; and that, in fact, our individual willingness to awaken prepares all of us to greet a new dawn. We are all bodhisattvas! We have come into these lives, these bodies, in order to find our way home. There is only one of us, and we are all working together to achieve our collective Moksha.

spiritual

As physical Moksha taught us about transcending the limitations of being in a body, and mental Moksha was about transcending the limiting beliefs we have agreed to, spiritual Moksha teaches us to transcend our attachment to how we think life should be. The Yoga Sutras of Patanjali offer us a path to our liberation through a method called Raja yoga. Sri Patanjali has taught us a practice which includes values and ethics, control of the body, breath and senses, meditation, and finally absorption into oneness, so that we might know, and become one with, our true selves.

Ramana Maharishi taught us that self inquiry is the fastest path to Moksha. From these two teachers we realize that to achieve Moksha we must quiet the fluctuations of our mind in order that we might uncover, and escape from, the confusing impulses of our transient human experience.

Extended visits into wild places in nature allow us to let go of our beliefs about ourselves, and show us that our self-identity is not all of who we are. When we release the attachments to our cultural lives by immersing ourselves into a world that doesn't revolve around cars and telephones, e-mail, media, or have and have-nots, we begin to see that we are more than what we have accumulated in this lifetime. Spending an extended period of time in the wilderness allows us to understand that we are truly interconnected with the life around us. There's no place superior to nature where we can learn that life itself is transient and ever-changing; that the changes are, in fact, life happening. Stationary life is not life, it isn't sentient, it isn't dynamic, and it isn't alive. To be alive requires change. Our liberation comes from seeing the changes occurring in our life as progress, rather than as something to fear and resist.

We must learn to lean into our lives, regardless of whether it pleases us. Human life is filled with sorrows and joys, and these changes happen all the time. If we only lean into life when it is joyful and hold back when we are grieving we never grow. When my son was murdered a few years ago I didn't know what to do. The only thing that I did know was to stay present. Whenever I tried to recoil or resist, sorrow would wash over me in ways I can't even describe. But when I was able to find it within myself to reach into my sorrow, when I would allow myself to touch the wound in some way, that would be the very moment when I would find healing. I have found that volunteering as a chaplain for local law enforcement agencies has allowed me to touch that wound in a profound way. I know what it means to lose someone important, and that knowing allows me to be with other families as they learn of the loss of their loved ones.

Even if you can't welcome the changes that happen in your life it's still vital that you accept them and the potential for personal and spiritual growth that you will find within them. One of the main lessons I learned from my son's death was that I now have an intimate connection with all mothers who have lost a child. There have been many times since his death that I've met other women whose child has passed from one cause or another, and yet somehow we know each other. It's as if we belong to an exclusive club where we know a secret that nobody else understands. I learned a significant lesson in being human; and it is my sorrow, to some extent, which defines my humanity. Joy is easy; it's easy to love each other through joyful times. It is easy to be open and accepting when your heart is filled with thoughts of love and bliss, but we grow more fully into love when we can be equally present during times of joy as well as during those times of sorrow.

In the Guru Gita we learn that the Guru is everything, including God. The Guru shines light into the corners of our darkness. It is the Guru who removes our spiritual ignorance wherein we believe that we are separate from God. For it is only in the realization that we are one with God that we find liberation. The Guru Gita teaches us to manifest perfection in all that we do. For it is in this realization of our inherent perfection that we express and realize our divinity.

While we might think of perfection as something, some goal, just out of our reach, perfection is simply doing the best we can in whatever situation we find ourselves. How could perfection ask anything more of us than that?

Living a life of efficiency allows us to spend more of our time in the practice of liberation. Wasting our time, wasting our efforts, creating karma and samskaras, does nothing to help us achieve Moksha. If we are busily caught up in the day to day dramas of life then our attention must remain in the mundane, asking us the question of whether we will be serving God, or Caesar. Because that's really what the question is: will you spend your time taking care of the daily, transient, illusory manifestations of human life, or will you spend your time seeking to realize the Self? One choice keeps you caught up in the cycle of life, while the other allows you to transcend the world of objects and their relationships. One choice leads to more sorrow and joy, while the other liberates you from the illusion of impermanence.

Synergy is a word that means more than the sum of its parts. Any condition we find ourselves in is comprised of any number of aspects and perspectives. Some of these are known to our conscious mind, others are hidden behind the concealing veil of our experiences, beliefs, culture, and the limitations of being in a body. As jiva, we are limited to what we can see by what may be seen in the physical experience of our lives. We only have a partial understanding of some of the circumstances in any given situation. Karma, our own egos, and the experiences and beliefs from our past lives are some of the things we probably do not have a full and complete understanding of.

I find it helpful to remember that I am not required to know everything, my soul has a direct connection to the Divine Mind, and that greater consciousness knows all that can be known. Staying open to wisdom teachings from current day and all the way back into antiquity, reminds me that life is taking care of itself and that if I can remember to remain open to insight and inspiration, and present in my day-to-day life experience, then I can rest in the knowledge that each moment is unfolding towards a greater and greater good for all.

In our study of Dharma we learned to recognize and follow our purpose in life, to be mindful of our activities and our thoughts. We learned of the practice of karma yoga through the lessons of the Bhagavad Gita. We discovered that we are interdependent beings living according to divine law, and we came to the realization that life is more than sequences of our personal experience.

Dharma teaches us to live on purpose, to respond rather than react, and that our true support comes from within. We learned the value of living with integrity and in harmony with all of life, causing us to consider our vocation, and our own place in the greater cosmology of humanity.

Artha offers us an understanding of the resources available to us. The fulfillment of this goal allows us to understand that we have everything we could possibly need available to us in any given moment. We learned of the six forms of wealth, and that wealth requires a greater responsibility to our family and community.

We learned that Artha is only a temporary reliever of suffering, and that life will always demonstrate what is in our consciousness. We discovered that we must give in order to receive, and that the real meaning of Artha is defined by the offerings we lay at the feet of God.

Kama teaches us that our desires must be filled or they will follow us into our next lives. Many of our desires are, in fact, a direct result of believing that we are separate from God. We learned that Kama is an exploration into opposites, and that when we believe we don't have something it is the belief itself that causes us to make choices which do not serve our greatest good and keep us apart from our desire. We defined pure versus impure desires, how we hurt ourselves through our actions and choices, and we learned how to bring our desire into balance.

Moksha is the transcendence of earthly life in order that we might experience spiritual freedom. It is the dance of Shiva and Shakti as they eternally spin through the universe. We discovered clues to finding our enlightenment within a physical body, the importance of setting goals, and that ultimately we want to worship everyone. For our greatest goal is to worship all of life.

It is through faith and devotion to the lessons and teachers we have found here that we find fulfillment of the Purusharthas; without Bhakti and Sraddha, devotion and faith, we will drift along haphazardly through our lives.

I offer this work to my ancestors, my teachers, and to my Divine Mother who never ceases to teach and entertain me in the most amazing of ways.

om shanti, shanti, shanti

Resources

Tomar, Vikrama A., "Ayurveda Four Aims of Life"

http://www.ayurveda-textbooks.com/ayurveda-four-aims-of-life.html (June, 2011)

Paulose, "Four Goals of Ayurvedic Life"

http://healthmad.com/alternative/four-goals-of-ayurvedic-life/ (July, 2011)

Vijayamohan, V., "Ancient Indian classification of human goals"

http://wisespiritualideas.blogspot.com/2010/06/human-goals-ancient-indian-system.html (June, 2011)

V, Jayaram, "Purusharthas or The Four Aims in Life"
http://www.hinduwebsite.com/hinduism/h_aims.asp
(June, 2011)

V, Jayaram, "The Arthashastra of Kautilya"

http://www.hinduwebsite.com/history/kautilya.asp

(July, 2011)

Easwaran, Eknath. *The Bhagavad Gita.*

    Berkeley, California: Nilgiri Press, 1998

Frawley, David. *Advanced Yoga & Ayurveda Course.*

Santa Fe, New Mexico: American Institute of Vedic Studies. 1986

Saraswati, Swami Satyananda. *The Chandi Path.*

Napa, California: Devi Mandir Publications, 2001

Saraswati, Swami Satyananda. *The Guru and the Goddess.*

Napa, California: Devi Mandir Publications, 1995

Yukteswar Giri, Jnanavatar Swami Sri. *The Holy Science.*

Los Angeles, California: Self Realization Fellowship, 1990